From Dreams, Through Wrestlings, To Fulfillment:

Poems of Growth

Journal Pages Included

By: Jennifer C.W. Gillyard

Author's Website: www.jenngillyard.com

Cover Design By: CB Creates, LLC www.cbcreates.org

Edited By: Megan Brinsfield, CPA and Author of My Life without Limits Blog

www.mylifewithoutlimits.com

authorHOUSE®

AuthorHouse™
1663 Liberty Drive
Bloomington, IN 47403
www.authorhouse.com
Phone: 1-800-839-8640

First published by AuthorHouse 9/6/2011

ISBN: 978-1-4567-6164-6 (e)
ISBN: 978-1-4567-6166-0 (sc)

Library of Congress Control Number: 2011907994

Printed in the United States of America

Any people depicted in stock imagery provided by Thinkstock are models, and such images are being used for illustrative purposes only. Certain stock imagery © Thinkstock.

This book is printed on acid-free paper.

From Dreams, Through Wrestlings, To Fulfillment provides the reader with words to stir insight and journal pages to encourage meditation and writing. This book of poetry includes five themed chapters capturing lively words of passion, sacrifice, and growth that will allow you, the reader, to experience an emotional journey with me. Blank journal pages, entitled "Veins of Inspiration" are inserted at the end of each chapter and include some of my very own quotes as well as my favorite quotes from biblical texts, inspirational leaders and authors that will help readers analyze public issues, process private thoughts and transcribe their feelings concerning life lessons. The title "Veins of Inspiration" was inspired from the thought of a vein being a transporting vessel for blood to flow to the heart, consequently providing the heart with life. For this author, the essence of life is synonymous with a burst of light or inspiration.

So come on a journey with me, take one poem at a time, acknowledge the emotion it provoked, and then reflect on your own experiences.

Enjoy!

Table of Contents

Wisdom & Advocacy

Family, Friend or Foe

A Voyage to Love

A Spiritual Dialogue

Sundry Thoughts

Me in a Nutshell

Jennifer

Outgoing, Sweet, Looney

Daughter of Larry

Lover of Church, School, and Wrestling

Who feels dizzy all the time, sick and optimistic about everything

Who fears stupidity, lack of self-control, and adulthood

Who would like a car, an acceptance letter from Harvard,

and Albert Einstein's brain

Resident of the City of Brotherly Love

Gillyard

@ 1997

A Dedication

To the one who stands and walks steadily at my four corners,
my instrument of direction.
To the one who stops the turning in circles and sets me on a linear path,
down a long paved road.
Not to the one who throws pebbles and sticks at my feet,
but to the one who tells me to skip along with joy.
To the one who lights a candle when my eyes are strained and heavy,
not to the one who blows out my light.
To the one on whom I lose focus and turn to walk an unpaved road.
Not to the one who only wants a piece of me,
but to the one whose whole heart I break daily.
To the one who searches for me patiently,
not the one who leaves me deserted and confused.
To the one whose suffering soaked long in tears,
for you chose to rescue me.
You give kind words, yet gentle discipline to experience my love and success.
It is only for you I get up when I stumble, only for you I seek understanding,
ONLY FOR YOU, I SERVE LONG.

To my parents: You carried me in your illness, so I vow to carry you in my strength and weakness. Thank you for your encouragement, love and maintaining our family structure. Psalms 73:24-26(NLT) states, "You guide me with your counsel, leading me to a glorious destiny. Whom have I in heaven but you? I desire you more than anything on earth. My health may fail, and my spirit may grow weak, but God remains the strength of my heart; he is mine forever."

Dedicated to:
Jennifer Chistina Witherspoon Gillyard

Love Child

J- For the JOY you have brought to your father and I, though you were once the bundle of tenderness, you are now the star of our eyes.

E- For the EMPTYNESS that was a scar in my heart, for the long years you have now filled.

N- Is for the NECESSITIES of life that you will in need of. We will always be there for you.

N- Is for NOURISHING you with so much love that you will never run out, it's a lifetime guarentee.

I- For INTERNAL keepsake, you are Gods gift to us, youare also His.

F- FORGET us not, for you are one in a million.

E- EVERLASTING love.

R- We Don't REGRET ~~ ever having you. We love you.

LOVE FROM US ALWAYS

Daddy &   Mommy

Jamillah Danielle W. Gillyard 7/18/75
Jonathan   Lee   W. Gillyard 3/30/77
Lydia   Gillyard 8/26/75
Jennifer Christina W. Gillyard 1/24/84

By Mother

WISDOM

&

ADVOCACY

A pen and some paper

A pen and some paper that's all I need
to cursive my thoughts on a graphed canvass,
thoughts accompanied with directional drawings,
I leave for you a planned legacy.

With a pen and some paper,
I distinguish when to capitalize a thought
then humbly lowercase that thought.
I know when to punctuate my end and
when to comma for breath,
then let my thoughts continue.
I leave for you a prudent legacy.

A pen and some paper,
with an understanding that white-out
although an option is not the solution
when it causes you to return to your mistakes.
Keep writing, keep learning, and move forward.
I leave for you a legacy of persistence.

A pen and some paper that's all I need
to write down my paragraphs of thoughts
leaving you an essay for life.

A New Day

Sun's rays on eyelids
spectrum of colors extracted from the mind
the Divine heating my soul to say
this is a new day.

Lay side-by-side - look up!
It's an elephant, no a giraffe!
Pictionary with my ancestors,
I chuckle. This is a new day.

Fresh air to breathe;
I skip and stumble on unpaved walkways,
the man greeted me and gave his coat as a walkway.
This indeed is a new day.

My people, in reply they say,
"What's up my sister?"
"My brother how have you been?"
Conversations of love and empowerment spring forth.
Be strong for today is a new day.
Belts once on a tree,
now around their waist;
thy son and daughter,
come mercy, over here grace.
Family eating at the dinner table
with words painting stimulated stories
across the membrane,
this is a new day.

Good afternoon my neighbor,
have you seen my child?
"She went to the corner store; my eyes are wide."
Those who have made the corner their deteriorating home
have been kind and know nothing they can offer us,
still they ponder He they can accept.
This is a new day.

Officer good night.
"Need a hand ma'am?"
No thank you.
He said he would remember my path, that's all I asked.
Yes, this world now is with me as I lay.
Tomorrow is a new day.

4

The Chore of One

I'm pissed off!

"Don't you speak that language," mama scorns.

My bad, I digress and rewind,

I'm pissed off!

Like a hound dog, I fold my ears to shut out the vapors you spit,

words of nonsense clotting my brain cells.

He said, she said crap. Won't you come out and play.

Let me be, be to myself for a day.

Taking on your cares and theirs,

his and her manuals have I none, just the common sense of one.

Pressure on me to clean up, speak here, help this one, work there,

oh and take time for yourself. Even I become a task to manage.

Everyday another drama, mama I'm sorry I have to explain.

I've lain down and I can't take others' pain any longer.

I refrained from howling my discontent, but hear me roar!

Let me be, free my mind from your insanity.

Teach yourself answers to the stupid questions you raise.

No offense, but I'm tired of this.

Adults with immature attitudes,

dude throw adolescence out the window.

Until you learn to grow up and become your own responsibility,

let me be.

Justice for All

When I am walking down the street, what do you see? A person, place, thing, or maybe I am just non-existing. What color comes across your mind? Is it black, white, yellow, or even polka dot. But is my color a reason to have me shot- I think not. Why can't you respect me for me, come on now let us face reality, I may not know you personally, but that is not a reason for me to tell you to leave my presence. Someday I hope you will agree, for this message will set many free from gangs and structured poverty. So let go of the hate, the hurt, and shame for I am not the one to blame. One day when our hearts come together to unite, you will see that I am right. Until then allow righteousness to set our lives aflame with love. Love overcoming fights, for justice is the greatest form of might. So are you ready? I am. Let us get on board, you never know when we'll miss our united flight.

Power of the Positive Mind

Catch a falling star, don't put it in your pocket.

Place it back in the sky and follow it.

Don't allow anyone to knock you off track.

Heart not the words of condemnation; solve the word problem with the

Word not the world.

You can do it.

Speakers of I can't best to rearrange words into I can.

Doubts fade like clouds parting across the sky,

particles of hope join larger clusters, for there is power in numbers.

Enemies spitting vocabulary of failure, however my heart simply itches

instead of burn.

You can do it for you.

I will defend my enemies, build them shelter even in harsh rain.

I will cry for the hurt and lost, pray for the forgotten and angry.

A child said God has a blanket that covers the whole land.

His love brings renewable peace and security to all, so I choose to love all.

A positive mind vows to serve, protect and re-do until accomplished.

It will love without fear of rejection and

love in rejection.

You can do it for them.

The positive mind stands firm and finds quietness with armed forces surrounding it.

When cast out into a deserted sea, it swims through waves of Calvary.

The positive mind continues to reach to help you with its left hand as you cut its right.

The power of the positive mind is the delivering

power of self-sacrifice.

Stay on track.

Dream for a Generation

Pressing up against the forces, I cry dry buckets of sympathy

Sympathy lacking compassion to relieve you from your pain

Pain of bringing forth a drug addicted generation

Generation of hate and separateness

Separateness of image giving cause for fighting

The American way learned from the selfish American Dream

No, our dream is one of unity, love, and survival

Our dream is respirating with King's remembrance

King, the healer of generations through wet buckets of compassion

Producing empathetic listening and communities empowered to mobility and change

Change that releases a drug addicted generation

Generation of many, but it took one to start the change

Change is You

You and I combined is we in number can make the Dream more effective

Effective is we can revive the Dream on life support

Support the lives of our youth

Youth, a new generation needing the Dream of a community

Questions

The sweat, the tears, the pain, I'm even ashamed to call out God's name. Who am I? What am I? Could I be lesser than that man who beats me around the clock, or am I lesser than the dirt in which flowers bloom, for in me nothing will ever bloom except the sorrow that brings me gloom.

While crying out to God, my tears glistening like the sun in the sky, these salty tears burn my eyes and make me realize what else is there to do than die. The confession I hold dear is too hard to bear no one would really care.

They only care about the time their next whipping will occur. So you can say I'm still alone, no freedom, therefore no place to go. I can't wait till the day I would hear my master say come and join me for a meal, instead of come and pay your whipping bill. I really can't say what my life means to me, but being a slave is reality, though forever more will I ask who am I and what is my purpose?

These are my questions.

Uncover Me

Like a thunderous cloud,

I tear drops of water.

A curtain has fallen on this beam of light.

Voice suffocating in cloudiness,

In darkness, I strain a song to disrupt the sun.

Awake, bring clarity, calm my fear with the relief you bring.

Illuminating shadow, uncover me and protect my shell,

help me to appear well.

Stress That Conquers

Mirrors often reveal myself to me

facial scars are so deep my pain you see.

My life is drowning in my confusion.

To give up hope is that my conclusion?

Happiness to me is an illusion.

Is depression thee only solution?

God help me to survive this life I live;

for hurting others and I, Lord forgive.

But it's stress that conquers me everywhere.

And my face shows all the things I had to bear.

Though in rough times I change my expression,

a phony smile in every direction.

Mirror, mirror on the wall look at me,

tell me, will my face ever seem care free.

Who Do I Say That I Am?

I am a theologian,
A Martin Luther running from the shadows of shame,
constantly calling on God's name
asking, "When will I sin no more?"
Chasing the gift of God's grace and
leaning not on my own understanding-
not even faith, for it's a gift.

I am a philosopher,
A Karl Marx, vigorously I fight for the uprisings of the poor
and the tearing down of political chains around our feet.
I write about a true democracy, where all are free.
Where different ethnic groups can enter schools and be able to compete-
with equal opportunity.

I am a social worker, a teacher-
A Jane Addams, one who says- come immigrants, come children, come poor,
come illiterate, come jail birds, come whores- your labels mean nothing to me.
Here's your shelter, here's your bread,
here's a safe place to lay your head.
And when you wake up, let us practice reading to one another
about a God who is our father and our mother.

I am an advocate,
A Martin Luther King, one whose voice rises
with every firm step towards integration and inclusion.
Nonviolent admonition to change your ways and social status delusions,
redirecting your efforts for the good of others.

The scripture said- Let this mind be in you...
Whose mind?
The mind of the righteous or the mind of the sick?
But are the sick really sick when they hold the gay teen's hand from committing
suicide and accept him as a human life force?

Are the sick really sick when they cry
for the pregnant women excommunicated from the church?
Are the sick really sick when they save the front pews of the church
for street walkers, orphans, pimps, widows, and homeless persons?
Are the sick really sick when they request inculturation in a worship service?

You preachers, why do you remain inside?
Why do you say that's not your calling?
Your ministry is at the door, in the street
from which you were first called at Calvary.
It is not on the front row appearing amicable
and holding a Bible,
which by the way looks too neat.

Exuding compassion, I stand alongside with the marginalized
and I will lead them across the border of the Church.
Will you accept them?
One can argue that care is relative,
but Jesus, not Paul or the disciples, was clear.
Who will you choose to follow?
I embody servitude... service is what I do...service is who I am.

Enclosed

Let me remain within, let no light come in,

taller, morph yourself, be broad not too thin.

Curls that cover the moon keep my thoughts from pushing out,

stay in, stick, and remain in that place;

within my bark I remain.

Dark, long, cold path now a shelter, no growth will occur,

here eyes have no pupils, body has no cords of contact.

Shhh! Dreams stand still.

Heart lock your door to sleep for a moment.

Volcanic crust under eye lids, cheeks pushing back tears.

A naked trunk separated from the weight of branches, leaves and tug of roots,

I stand alone,

within my bark I remain.

Delicate as the petal of a lily

Delicate as the petal of a lily
you wither onto your knees to pray for protection from
his rains of wrath.
Fires of insecurity melting your self-esteem to raise your tip with other lilies,
you regurgitate cries of care and need with a hand requesting redemption.
He condemns in fear with threats piercing your mind and bleeding heart with
questions of his everlasting affection.
Someone throw in the towel, this fight is too hard to bear alone, circling the ring in
panic search of a lover who has barricaded you in the walls once a home now a prison.
Someone slam the gavel on the concrete covering your heart once a garden of life and
fruitfulness now a ditch of anger and regret.
One songwriter demanded R-E-S-P-E-C-T another cried FREEDOM!
But with one bitter touch you lost both, your freedom no longer recognizable without the
reconciliation of respect and sense of worth that was taken when you were plucked from
your roots of stability, your foundation of growth, your belief in a love through every
season.
Storms screamed louder, your voice became softer, his became harsher.
The suns rays became unbearable, his action scorching, your petal brittle.
Delicate as the petal of a lily,
you fell when struck by his thunderous sky.
You pondered in your flight before the count of ten,
Where is the earth that brought me forth... I need you now.

Life is it worth it?

To me life was always worth living, for last night before I laid down I was a Jew, I had a name, a family, and a job or two. But this day I woke up to morning's glory and all I could see was Hell's great fury. I was scared, confused believing God had forsaken His people. Soldiers marching two by two searching families houses, taking all we owned, jewelry, money, even the clothes off our back and leaving us in the dirt foreseeing no bright future , just the colors of shame – red and black. We all were taken to camps to live and slave; we each were given a number to replace our names. I cried "why God, why are we being punished for being Jewish if we are your people", was my daily questioning. The answers to my questions were never given, leaving me in spiritual poverty. I would not have expected to survive this thing they called a Holocaust, for destruction is what it meant. Though last night, before I laid down, I had no name, no job and no family for they were dead. However, this day I woke up to morning's glory, and Hell had frozen over. Now with a burden of loss and feeling of hopelessness, I must tell a new story, one about a life that seeks to mend around the scars.

Don't Hold Back

Scream your purpose, who you will be.

Let it be known to everyone you meet on the street, see out the window,

Declare your name in the NY Times, put your eulogy in the Washington Post.

When my spirit is set free, this is me.

Speak before your time, your places your things.

Unearth that which you've visualized and present it to the heavens.

Howl like the owl, cockatoo like the roster.

Wake the world and make them respond to your call.

Arise, gift inside of you don't you dare sit in thy belly,

I ate the scroll of life's directions and God has paved the way.

So I speak to your gift and say arise and walk with me on this journey to set others free.

My call has been heard in the mind during the night, I responded hear I come.

Who will follow me and join the band of restored instruments,

Stomping the ground of ruins -

Don't hold back,

Someone needs to hear this sound of freedom and victory,

Don't Hold back.

This is for my children who have been forgotten by their families and the government,

Don't Hold Back.

This is for the sibling dying from HIV,

Don't Hold Back.

This is for the abandoned homes left in our communities to look at while homelessness pervades the streets,

Don't Hold Back.

This is to make spirituality gender neutral,

Don't Hold Back.

I'm still frustrated when you consider me less than because of the color of my skin,

Don't Hold Back.

For families on welfare, placed in a cyclical economic process of despair,

Don't Hold Back.

This is for the children who suffer within poor and underfunded educational systems,

Don't Hold Back.

I'm tired of listening to party platforms that don't care about holistic approaches to preserving the human race,

Don't Hold Back.

Tear down the prisons that don't practice rehabilitation,

Don't Hold Back.

Change the law that won't give "Rehabilitated" individuals the right to vote or apply for educational assistance to advance themselves,

Don't Hold Back.

The American Dream has not paid us due rights, so why are we allowing it to inhabit within us. The Dream becomes American once we exercise our voices and receive our rights as a diverse yet unified people,

Don't Hold Back.

Put a stretcher of faith between you and I as we glide and bring back the hope of we shall overcome.

Now being awake and united, let's not close our eyes, but dream on our toes and raise our hearts to the sky.

Lord rain on us a Dream for a new generation without broken families and washed away communities. We stand together as one, ready to receive individual purpose for a communal restoration.

My purpose is revealed once again, I am renewed with my brothers- hang tough, empowered with my sisters - hold on.

The journey is long, but the vision has been made clear.

Write it down for the news anchor, graffiti the message on the sides of buildings.

Put your arms within mine as we align and walk, being guarded with armor slicing through identity crisis and separate yet equal boundaries.

We are the people with purpose to initiate the plan.

Ready, Set, Calling all Warriors- It's Time to fight, Don't Hold Back.

Veins of Inspiration

_____
_____
_____
_____
_____
_____
_____
_____
_____
_____
_____
_____
_____
_____
_____
_____
_____
_____
_____
_____
_____
_____

*"My heart aches for world deliverance and my blood now
pours freely releasing the clot of violence."*

Veins of Inspiration

_____

_____

_____

_____

_____

_____

_____

_____

_____

_____

_____

_____

_____

_____

_____

_____

_____

_____

_____

_____

_____

_____

"Oh that you would bless me and extend my lands! Please be with me in all that I do, and keep me from all trouble and pain!" – 1 Chronicles 4:10 (NLT)

Veins of Inspiration

_____

_____

_____

_____

_____

_____

_____

_____

_____

_____

_____

_____

_____

_____

_____

_____

_____

_____

_____

_____

_____

_____

"Progress is never idle."

Veins of Inspiration

"The greatest feeling is the crack of the heart at the cry of destitution."

"You fasten your heart to everyone that would fall without your support."

_____
_____
_____
_____
_____
_____
_____
_____
_____
_____
_____
_____
_____
_____
_____
_____
_____
_____
_____
_____

"It's less about who you are in the world and more about who you are in action."

Veins of Inspiration

_____
_____
_____
_____
_____
_____
_____
_____
_____
_____
_____
_____
_____
_____
_____
_____
_____
_____
_____
_____
_____
_____
_____
_____

"The worst illness is not leprosy or tuberculosis, but the sense of being unwanted, of not being loved, of feeling abandoned." – Mother Teresa

Veins of Inspiration

_____

_____

_____

_____

_____

_____

_____

_____

_____

_____

_____

_____

_____

_____

_____

_____

_____

_____

_____

_____

_____

"Stop wearing your wishbone where your backbone ought to be."
– Elizabeth Gilbert (Eat, Pray, Love)

"With God a missed opportunity is called a boomerang."

Veins of Inspiration

"To obtain wisdom means to inform oneself. To show wisdom means to act in understanding." – Based on Proverbs 4:7-8

Veins of Inspiration

_____

_____

_____

_____

_____

_____

_____

_____

_____

_____

_____

_____

_____

_____

_____

_____

_____

_____

_____

_____

_____

"The only thing worst than being blind is having sight but no vision."
– Helen Keller

Veins of Inspiration

"The best method of self-defense is knowledge, not fists."

_____

_____

_____

_____

_____

_____

_____

_____

_____

_____

_____

_____

_____

_____

_____

_____

_____

_____

_____

_____

_____

"Happiness is not a goal; it is a by-product." – Eleanor Roosevelt

Veins of Inspiration

_____

_____

_____

_____

_____

_____

_____

_____

_____

_____

_____

_____

_____

_____

_____

_____

_____

_____

_____

_____

_____

"Wisdom hears the eternal heart not the temporary."

Veins of Inspiration

"The weapon is loaded with your head down, while the
mind is loaded with the head facing upward."

_____

_____

_____

_____

_____

_____

_____

_____

_____

_____

_____

_____

_____

_____

_____

_____

_____

_____

_____

_____

"A soldier in armor is as worthless without a weapon as is a Christian with a Bible and no faith. Faith is your weapon."

Veins of Inspiration

"The weight of all memories will cause you to fall backwards."

Veins of Inspiration

_____
_____
_____
_____
_____
_____
_____
_____
_____
_____
_____
_____
_____
_____
_____
_____
_____
_____
_____
_____
_____

"Don't let anyone think less of you because you are young."
– 1Timothy 4:12 (NLT)

Veins of Inspiration

"We love because it's the only true adventure." – Nikki Giovanni

Veins of Inspiration

_____
_____
_____
_____
_____
_____
_____
_____
_____
_____
_____
_____
_____
_____
_____
_____
_____
_____
_____
_____
_____
_____

*"A wise minister listens to and joins hands with world religions
to bring peace to nations. A foolish minister closes both ears and
hands towards world religions bringing violence to nations."*

Veins of Inspiration

_____
_____
_____
_____
_____
_____
_____
_____
_____
_____
_____
_____
_____
_____
_____
_____
_____
_____
_____
_____
_____
_____

"Chase the dream, the people will fall into place."

_____

_____

_____

_____

_____

_____

_____

_____

_____

_____

_____

_____

_____

_____

_____

_____

_____

_____

_____

_____

"Transformation deals not with a change, rather your level of strength."

"Failure does not mean the vision is dead, it means the vision is being renewed."

FAMILY,
FRIEND
OR
FOE

He Is You...

He is you...
He is the man in the kitchen stirring up a pot of creative goodness
to nourish a blended family
once broken by bitterness, he restores as he sweeps broken pieces from off the floor
and helps build new bridges across forgiveness to love.
He carries a rough, cracked stone and at times allows a river to flow through it
supplying others with a renewed sense of being.
His words soaking down through your heart's scarred material
reminds your spirit of purpose, as he uses strength to fix the purpose of worldly objects.
He is the man that keeps me on the wheel of creation,
creating living art through intelligent movement.
He taught me to create through sacrifice.
He gave half to make the whole- whole family, whole mind, and whole future- He gave.

He gave what You are...
Solid rock on which I stand, no solid rock on which I hold for protection and guidance
all other ground is sinking sand, thanking God for the wisdom he gave you to pass on to
me that I may withstand the trials from all forms of temptation.
How can I repay the man God allowed to walk through an enduring crucifixion of varying
emotions towards him from those he loves as well as begs and pleas from those he carries?
This is your calling- a father- a warrior- that is who you are.
You bare the scars of love, no amount of hugs or tears or praise can
re-do and return what you have done because it cannot be measured.
Truth and mercy hang from your shoulders; you lift us out of darkness into the light
within your eyes that say "I will never leave."
Body weary from a 24-hour workday, living and giving life is your job.
I only pray for your strength to see the days we take off and play.
Even in your absence, you are present,
your voice of wisdom resounding loudly in my ear to give direction.
You maintain this family in health and love,
you are God's alter ego of strength through tough love.
I pray you will only see that the love you have for me and this family
is gladly given in return with no holds barred.
We grip life with both hands along side of you ready for every journey with you
not yet after, though your legacy will be so fruitful.

We are because He is...

He is the personal walking heart of an all-access, distant spirit God.

He is my father, my dad, my best friend, my example of God as man,

an example of man as husband and an example to those who need to see a changed man.

He is more than enough; he is the manuscript on fatherhood.

He is a gentle love, a kind love, a love that provides, a love that endures,

a love that suffers long, and a love that never grows weary...

He is You.

Lucky

You were given in exchange for a book,
a book on expressing love.
She surprised me with you,
showing the love of a best friend.
You in a gray tee-shirt, and
yellow vest with a hoodie attached,
reminded me of her calm tomboy style.
The symbol on your sleeve is a four-leaf clover,
though on the same side a symbol
in the form of Pooh is indented in her arm.
Big, round, brown eyes,
a nose made out of brown string,
resembles her brown cubby face and body,
with the cutest ornaments as facial features.
Your soft brown fur that looks as if shampoo
was left on your body to soak reminds me
of her wild, squishy locks.
Holding you makes my tossing night times
smoother. Being with her helps me get
through many rough times.
Gift from a gift, your name is no mistake,
for I am lucky to have the friend
from which you came.

OZ

Out from a scarred womb
into a cruel world,
premature, small crown
I was nothing crowding your air.
Though unlike the cowardly lion,
I have courage,
so I'm coming out.

Grown, but not my body,
Laugh at me why don't you.
Smidget, Pinocchio, Troll,
I hear your voices.
Extra cartilage in spine and nose,
walking side ways with three eyes they say,
and straight pointed toes.
But unlike the scarecrow,
intelligence tells me
I'm coming out.

The stories and backbiting never cease.
My friend, rape my soul again with your
"I love you" and "Of course we do."
Hello, unlike the tin man, I have a heart.
Talk your dislike about me
through your teeth,
until my name has its own heart beat.
But if I allow you to stop me,
I would die,
So I'm coming out.

Now watch me as I pass by
with my hand in God's holding life's desires.
Snatching my name off the tip of your tongue,
and restoring my pride, my soul, my life.
Yes, I forgive you,
cause unlike Dorothy in God I have a home.
Now look closely, cause life like a whisper
will propel me by and
from out of your wicked pain and into my gain,
I'll break the chains and deafen my ears to your words.
Finally I'm coming out.

A Mutt

Don't call me what you think I am, for what you think I am- I am not. I know the first thing you see when you look at me is the color of my skin, as black as Africa's women, but do not judge me by what you see, for what you see I am not. Race is not me, and culture is more than this family you see. I am 50% Black, should I be ashamed to call on the name of my ancestors? Moreover, I am Indian, 30% my friend. Whether Cherokee or Sioux, why do you bother with the issue- I am human like you. White, I can say I am 15%, which I am sure comes as a shock to you. Lastly, my 5% comes from being Puerto Rican. However, do you care this is my families blood lines running through my hair. A mutt you call me, well I do not think that is fair. I am 100% American, and that is my sum and the same Mother Nature has rained gain through my hands. Race is not me, and culture is more than this family you see; allow AMERICAN to shape my visibility.

Release the Pressure

During a study session,
being suffocated by the hundreds
of students sitting around me,
I started to breathe heavily.
I felt my heart expanding outwards as if it were gasping for air.
It felt like needles were grabbing and sucking on the veins of my heart,
as a leech would thirst upon its prey.
I quickly put both hands over my chest,
until my heartbeats became less punctuated,
I became frightened.
After the session I ran home,
only to find that terror had beat me to my room.
Ringing, the phone resounded like
thin metal needles hitting the ground in sequence,
I suffocated the receiver with both hands.
Then I heard it.
The pain in my chest had been the pain in my uncle's.
How could it be? He had been as healthy, harmless, and peaceful as a still lake.
Now his heart's currents were disrupted
as if someone were catapulting rocks of all sizes into it.
I wished I could be there with him,
our distance was making my heart hurt more.
I wanted to cry, but I could not for fear congested me.
Then in a moment's time, I began to feel my heart pump faster,
then faster, as if it were trying to conquer an impossible race.
It felt like life
      outracing
            death's suffocation.
                  Maybe this can be a sign of a winner by a heartbeat...

Have you seen her?

She's beauty in its very essence,
as lovely as the rising sunflower in spring.
Yet as fragile as the withering
rose petal in winter.
She's a Rahab draped in white,
but covered and bruised with love's afflictions.

She's like that sunflower's stem
that when displaced remains intact,
holding on to her roots.
She's an Ester, in poverty and suffering,
she can rise as protector and comforter of a nation.

She's the sunflower that sticks her neck out
to get God's attention through the sun's rays.
She's like a child yearning for His touch alone
to heal her and the world she alone seems to brighten.

She's life in all its pain, strength and passion,
she's a woman draped in sun burnt skin,
pushing through the crowd of tall, fair tulips.
She's the unknown woman with an issue of blood favored by God.
That one is virtuous; that woman is mother.

Time Travel

Memories as blood rush to the front of my brain:

In Women's Medical, I was small enough to fit
in my doctor's pocket.
With so many screams
from being exposed
to a cold world,
Larry and Cathy cradled me
in a pink animal-printed blanket,
where I dreamed and left this place behind.

I was officially a child and my body filled out.
My hair expanded in afro puffs that included foreign objects
from combs to gum and I recall it being a task for mother.
For every twitch from the comb, I would be smacked by the wooden brush.
She'd coldly grunt "you better stay still," through her false scary pasty teeth.
I was energetic, with calluses not on my heels, rather on my toes.
I always had to be fast enough to beat the two-inch high heel shoe
boomeranging up the stairs in my direction.
I ran to the protector who sternly objected "Don't you hit my baby."

Then it was time for high school,
which resembled Hell turned inside out.
The children from a cockeyed view appeared as angels,
some with wings both attached, others with one attached
and the other wing falling off.
I explored the reasons why girls with cold attitudes walked around
with painted faces, and why boys never found the time
to finish dressing in the morning.
My hormones became Mexican jumping beans, though I was controlled
by the ton of work that unfortunately sometimes tipped kids
off the ledge of the school's roof, I had that idea.

Now I'm here- college. I'm more excited than an electrocuted scalp.
Though confusion of direction soils my solid standing in life.
Classes are filled with geniuses- so I ask am I smart enough?
Students here mature so fast and soon I will ask- where did my youth go?

You dare call me a woman? Ma'am you say.
But I am only an inferior freshman with the same length
of stretched body as when I was a child,
though my hair is a little straighter now.

I'm becoming scared of my future.
It seems that my body has developed faster than my confidence.
What can I do without my mother's lectures through her teeth.
I want to see the boomeranging shoe again, but this time I won't run.
I need my pink animal-printed blanket,
but this time I will be too scared to grow up, so I refuse to dream.
What can I possibly do without my parents?

Gone but Not Forgotten

Write me something you say, why not speak of me.

Honestly, you left without a trace, memories of you running too freely,

that I must gather to decipher the poetry of your once existence.

Through your kin, I see you, through photos I feel you, at night I hear you still

laughing at my knock-knock jokes.

I miss you, all you left was a wounded friend I call mother and a distant son I sought

to call husband.

While on earth your silent presence was so strong yet you were a danger to yourself.

You leaving hit so hard and rang so loudly in our spirits.

You left without a trace and the earth shifted with you.

Write something you say, I ask if you loved me let me sense you again through my

earth.

My Sister Friend

(Written by Jennifer Gillyard and Sung by Christian Belton)

Out of the dust you were made behind Adam,

Standing there, working, healing while man rested or wandered

Even in constant motion, we were drawn together,

Connected not by biology rather by psychology.

We studied each other's ethic, demeanor, and need.

We sought to connect and meet each other's provisions, teaching man his

forthcoming task.

You became my friend…

(Melody to the tune of India Arie "There's Hope")

My friend,

Always there for me,

Always see me through,

No one like you

You know you're my friend

No matter what's going on

Call you up on the phone,

Tell you what's going wrong

Because you're my friend.

From fashion to accessories, you know it all.

You teach me how to stand, walk tall and dress, but not flaunt it all.

So this is to the one who taught me how to walk gracefully on my toes and pat my

nose.

To the one who said hair- let it flow, and shawl- that needs to go!

To the one who showed me the softer side of femininity.

To the one who said this looks nice, and put your bang to the right,

And –Girl, your skills are tight!

(Melody to the tune of Salt & Pepper "It's a She Thang")

Cause it's a she thang, and it's all in me,

I can be anything that I choose to be,

Don't consider me a minority,
Ladies help me out - if you agree- it's a she thang.

To the one who claims a great future, places, and things.
The only one I would admit- this is what I would want for a wedding ring.
My cares are mounted as your cares, for that's the Siamese way,
Leads us to reminisce about the Pisgah days.

Spirit intertwined in spirit together on earth we reign
You are my spirit's recommencement.
When I stood behind, you pushed me up front, when I went left you pushed me right
And said- You're worth more than mediocre.
You became my sister

(Melody to the tune of Angie Stone's "Black Brother")
Cause you're my black sister,
Strong sister, I'll never try to hurt ya.
I want you to know that I'm here for you
For whatever- truth.

To get to me you must go through her, my protector.
My eclipse, you defend my name from insults and back from stabbing.
Bleeding heart, even in silent conflict your actions show you forgave and forgot.

Clothed in purple, yet with stains of white
The world pulls on your spirit and you freely give and say it'll return back to me all I lend.
Support when drowning in tears of hurt, disappointment in love, fears of failure,
You remind me all I can ever do is WIN.

You became my sister friend

(Melody to the tune of Biz Markie's "Oh Baby You")
O, sister you
You got what I need
You are my sister friend

And you'll be there till the end,
O sister you,
Encourage me through
All the ups and downs
And you'll always be around
O, sister you.

When life falls apart like a piano with no legs- a heavy tune you sing for me.
Comfort in silence we hear the matters of each other's heart and internalize a
rhythmic prayer- A faithful hymn is you.
Head to head, toe to toe
The battles can only pass behind us.
We're armed in heart, shielded with purpose, chained in victory,
Reciprocating strength in the other's weakness.

Like Elizabeth and Mary, we subject ourselves to love and greatness.
So I call you sister: successful, initiator, sustainable, thoughtful, entity- are you.
And I call you friend: forever, reverent, in each, new, day, we share together sister
friend-
I AM.
And even if our path for a season reached a dead end, and one of us must make a
turn,
The earth will circle us back again to the true friend we've always known.
I'll always love you- my sister friend.

(Words and Melody by Whitney Houston's and Cece Winans' song "Count on Me")
"Count on me through thick and thin
A friendship that will never end
When you are weak, I will be strong
Helping you to carry on
Call on me I will be there
Don't be afraid,
Please believe me when I say count on
You can count on me."

_____
_____
_____
_____
_____
_____
_____
_____
_____
_____
_____
_____
_____
_____
_____
_____
_____
_____
_____
_____
_____

"People with integrity do what they say they are going to do. Others have excuses." – Laura Schlessinger

_____
_____
_____
_____
_____
_____
_____
_____
_____
_____
_____
_____
_____
_____
_____
_____
_____
_____
_____
_____
_____
_____

"Man is born broken. He lives by mending. The grace of God is the glue."
– Eugene O'Neill

"Once we accept our limits, we go beyond them." – Albert Einstein

Veins of Inspiration

"God can do anything, you know – far more than you could ever imagine or guess or request in your wildest dreams...." – Ephesians 3:20 (MSGV)

Veins of Inspiration

"One's spirit can be kept alive in the actions of their children."

Veins of Inspiration

"Quick! Catch all the little foxes before they ruin the vineyard of your love."
– Songs of Songs 2:15 (NLT)

_____
_____
_____
_____
_____
_____
_____
_____
_____
_____
_____
_____
_____
_____
_____
_____
_____
_____
_____
_____

"Tell me and I'll forget. Show me, and I may not remember. Involve me, and I'll understand." – Native American Saying

Veins of Inspiration

"Right now, therefore, every time we get the chance, let us
work for the benefit of all..." – Galatians 6:10 (MSGV)

Veins of Inspiration

"Mockers scorn that which they cannot obtain, a care-free presence."

Veins of Inspiration

"I was born for more than this!"
– Bruce Wilkinson (The Prayer of Jabez for Teens)

"Don't burn out; keep yourselves fueled and aflame..." – Romans 12:12 (MSGV)

Veins of Inspiration

"We may be surprised at the people we find in heaven. God has a soft spot for sinners. His standards are quite low." – Desmond Tutu

Veins of Inspiration

"Nothing, you see, is impossible with God." – Luke 1:37 (MSGV)

Veins of Inspiration

_____

_____

_____

_____

_____

_____

_____

_____

_____

_____

_____

_____

_____

_____

_____

_____

_____

_____

_____

_____

_____

_____

"I was inspired by Mary McLeod Bethune, not only to be concerned but to use whatever talent I had to be of some service in the community." – Dorothy Height

_____
_____
_____
_____
_____
_____
_____
_____
_____
_____
_____
_____
_____
_____
_____
_____
_____
_____
_____
_____
_____
_____
_____

"To lose balance sometimes for love is part of living a balanced life."
– Elizabeth Gilbert (Eat, Pray, Love)

Veins of Inspiration

"I know you inside and out, and find little to my liking. You're not cold, you're not hot-far better to be either cold or hot! You're stale. You're stagnant."
– Revelation 3:15-16 (MSGV)

Veins of Inspiration

"I've learned that people will forget what you said, people will forget what you did, but people will never forget how you made them feel." – Maya Angelou

_____

_____

_____

_____

_____

_____

_____

_____

_____

_____

_____

_____

_____

_____

_____

_____

_____

_____

_____

_____

_____

_____

"There is no house like the house of belonging." – David Whyte

Veins of Inspiration

"*Mockery is confused in the presence of laughter.*"

Veins of Inspiration

_____
_____
_____
_____
_____
_____
_____
_____
_____
_____
_____
_____
_____
_____
_____
_____
_____
_____
_____
_____
_____
_____

"I leave you love. I leave you hope, I leave you the challenge of developing confidence in one another. I leave you respect for the use of power. I leave you faith. I leave you racial dignity." – Mary McLeod Bethune

Veins of Inspiration

"I bless God every chance I get; my lungs expand with his praise."
– Psalms 34:1(MSGV)

Veins of Inspiration

_____
_____
_____
_____
_____
_____
_____
_____
_____
_____
_____
_____
_____
_____
_____
_____
_____
_____
_____
_____
_____

*"Focus on friends or love, you waste time. Time meant to
cultivate God's grace only you can show to the world."*

Veins of Inspiration

"No one can make you feel inferior without your consent." – Eleanor Roosevelt

_____

_____

_____

_____

_____

_____

_____

_____

_____

_____

_____

_____

_____

_____

_____

_____

_____

_____

_____

_____

*"I recognize the player. His motives are like cracks in the
concrete, narrow yet obvious and I still trip into it."*

Veins of Inspiration

"I prayed for twenty years but received no answer until I prayed with my legs."
– Frederick Douglas

A
VOYAGE
TO
LOVE

He Said

He said...
I want to be the friend whose chest you fall on when you get tired,
the one who cries with you when you get angry,
the friend who's allowed to kiss you when it's not a special occasion.

He said...
I want to be the friend to whom you can tell all your dreams and fears and feel secure,
the friend who bears the weight of your conversation from a hard workday.

He said...
I want to be the friend whose eyes you look into and hesitate to blink,
the friend who brings you breakfast in bed.
The friend who can hold you into slumber,
and in the morning wake God to ask, "can I see her one more day."

He said...
I just want us to be.

What's Love Got to Do With It?

Jump on, Jump off
rolling body on top of body
down the wet grassy hill.
You hold me tightly till our tips touch.
Giving each other the googly-eyed
frantic head motion that leads to a
kiss soliciting the eruption of my heart.
You caress my hair, my neck,
your hands roaming my outer parts,
their imprints on my skin yelling- let me inside.
Then I whisper "I love You,"
and you casually smile,
but my heart knows your type.
What's love got to do with it, you're thinking,
as you hear me panting from feeling
you going from base to base, pacing the homerun.
Well, at least I have someone who desires me – I reason.
But someone once said,
the greatest thing in life is to love
and be loved in return.
I try to push him away from drilling more
sexual frustration into my heart.
I tell him again "I love you."
His face becomes blank
as if his brain froze any line of thought.
I interject silence to say,
Love has everything to do with it.

The Unimaginable You

My heart has stopped.
Stopped beating for the hope,
the "what ifs",
and the thread width possibility of love.
Your love is stagnant, with impurity
of the eyes and mudslides of the brain.
I have to climb up and
leap over your hills of lies
and finger pointing immaturity.
If you do not want the responsibility,
then do not bother me!
If you never loved me,
then come no longer to tread on this territory.
I am tired of providing you
with unreciprocated care and conversation.
My heart beats to stand
and says this is not fair.
Though it may be hard to let you go,
I refuse to stretch out to the unimaginable,
that is having you.

A Daze

I can't breathe
breath on window
spreading midst
searching for that perfect love
that childhood fantasy
princess charming in pursuit
of her handsome prince
I wipe away the dew to see emptiness in view
no passerby looks this way
I ask God to calm the storms raging within
franticly looking for an earthly connector
waters submerge out from within
hope pressed down, fear running over
I ponder is it even meant for me.

The Art of Love Making

As the artist paints onto his canvas
your lips brush across my body.
Painting- that's his natural gift.
Clouds of kisses from head to toe,
tonight you are my prince and I sir am your pauper.
To make me whole, complete in beauty that is a woman,
silver and gold have you none,
but what you possess is far more wonderful.
I am a sunflower bowed in coldness,
sitting among a bed of standing roses.
You are my bee, nurtured in honey,
you grace me with a taste.
Every inch of my being rises on my flowerbed; I'm elevated in your warmth.
The earth takes pleasure as our bodies unite and become one.
The mountains sweat, the rivers run passionately
yet slowly to prevent running dry.
As the moon rests in fulfillment, the sun peeks with beaming desire.
You hold me and inscribe a kiss, leaving your signature on my body and in my heart.
Everyday you wipe the canvass clean
and paint a more colorful picture,
but always of the same object that has your affection.

My Closet

Hesitantly, yesterday I completely opened you,
and I felt that cool spring breeze
yet overcome by the summer scent of Germantown streets,
you allowed me to see us.

(Memory five years old)
You remember in the back of that old church van
we played games, played with our wrestling figures- I always won.
How we talked, laughed until
the adults warned us to calm down.
Oh and how she always dropped you off on weekends
to play or sleep if her nights ran long.

(Memory eight years old)
She died, I held on to Pisgah's doors but was pried away,
jumbled with sadness and care I was not allowed to enter in.
He feared I was too young.
I never saw you again.
You never called.
I missed my friend.
I missed her so much.
I prayed for you every night.

(Memory fifteen years old)
You were there,
at the same high school as me.
I thought we would rekindle the old times, years lost.
With your new crowd of friends
our past was a blank slate.
You wanted nothing to do with me,
not even my courtesy.

(Memory seventeen years old)
You came to church,

almost a grown man.
You said you were leaving for the Air Force,
I myself was leaving for the Army.
We joked, laughed, and said until next time...
My heart saluted you, as you again
walked out of my life for seasons at a time.

(Memory last night)
At the age of nineteen,
I have realized that you,
the one I considered my best friend
and wishful thinking- my first love,
had also left me at the age of eight.
But I continue to leave my closet door ajar.

My Imperfect Ideal

Cease ! Please go away, this heart has no home there

why be tempted with a distant view, now in the rear.

Don't slow down to watch, yet keep pushing forward towards your mark.

Heart don't hold on,

reaching out ~ I fall through a silhouette.

Similar clouds in two hemispheres of the sky following circles, no straight lines.

The heart is most powerful without its sight,

blinded by desire my mind is losing the fight.

Shut-up! Heart stop escalating.

My mind knows it's not right, it's not true,

only seen through HD.

You don't understand, thy hand blends in a crowd of hearts

as a fan circles sharply through dusty airs.

Back away, don't get cut. Go and breathe solo airs.

This is not the right hand, or heart to ponder.

Push the thought to fade as the sky colors the crescent moon black,

as a curtain hides the sunlight through the blinds.

I glimpse through a cracked opening with a bleached eye.

Falling in Love

Falling in love is like a smooth, winding road on a cliff; only the brave, focused and hopeful may survive. I was neither when it came to love.

I would fall on or for anything and anyone then slip back into a shell with a flickering of doubt.

But this was not supposed to happen; the owl never soars openly in the light.

You came in the night and pulled me into the day, held me as I tried to pull away.

You tripped me with your persistence and confused me with your lullaby of security and affection I thought I could avoid, until you held me and put all my fears at ease, I never could.

I looked into your eyes and saw a film holding back a river of tears creating a sparkle of desire and recognition of your spirit's ability to supply my needs.

My eyes smiled with joy and as you looked into my eyes, you cuffed my heart and held my chin in your palms.

During extended absences, my mind wanders every hour. I watch the clock as minutes snap, slowly pacing the seconds granting me more time to think of you.

Focused for a minute to complete daily tasks then I'm stopped in motion with a vision of you crossing my mind and with a smile waking my cheeks I think how lovely it would be to experience your caress; hunched over I throw myself back into my tasks.

We meet again, both of us scared to say those three words. You put your forehead to mine, tangle your fingers between mine and with a breath, you whisper, "I'm falling for you."

Four words that indicated the wheels of your heart are turning with mine.

Falling in love is like overcoming a fear, you won't know its power until you expose yourself.

I responded, "I am falling in love and hope this feeling never ends."

My Heart Takes A Bow

My heart is breaking, sadness exfoliating through my skin,

I rub the irritated sores left from sizzling conversation,

now only cratered flesh of awareness in being lost surrounded by deep confusion,

a scab forms over the wound you left.

It's either you lied or I heard the pauses in between your words saying, "I need you".

I lied to myself believing that you would protect, provide, and profess in the manner that

love from a man could be expressed.

Instead, I allowed you to disrupt, disgrace, and deny my role in your life.

The physical wounds will heal more quickly than the emotional,

when the heart breaks, it takes regular breaths to draw it back together.

My breath is gone, you took it along with the silence you left in.

The heart now stands at an obtuse angle with yours half-flat lined and mine struggling

to stand on its own,

no force holding the parts together, for the force was in the imagination of being needed

rather than rejected.

A Longing

Melodies...Melodies...
are my thoughts of you.
Imagining us dancing like the wind
makes me sway from side to side.
If you only knew how excited
my heart gets at the thought of you.
At the thought of your warm smile,
your masculine tone echoing into my soul
and melting my independence.
For I long to fly, dependent on you and our love
to guide me through this lonely world.
If you only knew how long I have awaited you.
Daydreaming of you has moved into my nights.
I try to let your youthful memory go,
yet the hope of your present manhood is so tangible.
I want to listen to God's voice,
overlooking the mountains and rivers with you.
My soul longs for you to whisper your heart, your plans, and your thoughts
to only me and pour out your love only for me.
I long to know you deeply and completely.
Every nerve in my body blushes at the vision of us
walking towards each other, discovering one another's hands.
Thinking of you, I will not cease until I see you and touch you.
I pause,
to hear our melody.

Faded Picture

Get a rise out of me, you're just a bloody glove,

the only evidence from your lies and deceitful eyes - turn around!

I despise you, no I despise me for being your totem post.

Being stepped on by the host of my heart, brain teaser,

you were just a masturbated thought.

Premature empty ejaculation issuing temporary pleasure from going through the motions.

However, get a rise out of me- Never!

I reject your erect stance of savior.

My needs are already fulfilled and confidence is my banner.

Walk on me tall no longer.

My greatest downfall was trying to pick you up.

Wisdom stems from lessons of life and love.

Suck on this bosom no longer to feed.

I labored my own path and I take responsibility for making you an option.

Now modern preferences are being framed in my mind,

your antique image has been relinquished to my past.

Lover's Cry

Unspeakable, unquenchable, desire to be loved.

But, by whom...

By someone untouchable, someone not confinable.

If the cords over my heart stretched any further they would break in pitch of my
love cry.

Images of one so true, pure, amusing, smart, and manly upset my reality for a moment
of a fantasy realized, a dream become reality, a future become present.

I know the smell of fantasy, a burning desire gone cold with the winds of reality pushing
me into another's arms, one not so true, pure, amusing, smart, or manly.

If I could just be in position to pass you by, exchange the words of a lover's cry,
would you respond with a glare, then a smile, and run with a steady pace to a child-like
face as my heart races.

Searching in suicide form for this love so true, pure, amusing, smart, and manly,
hands on knees, gasping for air I question if I will ever see you and have you see me
or am I destined to look through to you and
your eyes never seek me – here – in my position of life.

Feeling this hollowness in my belly, I hope you feel it too.

If you are hungry for true love, then come and dig
through unfamiliar soil to seek me.

Lord, deliver hearts unnoticed and turn our cry into a hymn of praise.

The Journey of Love

Love

Love is when I hear your name

Running through my veins like a melody

Up and down are my emotions on a chord

With every stare, every smile you simultaneously tug me closer and let me loose

Love

Love is the helium over my heart

Nervousness prevents my beat from reciprocating your touch of affection

You cradle me by your side

I close my eyes and fall away from the warmth of your security

You catch me with your eyes that say love never fails

Love

Love is a spirit stretched in distance and loud in silence.

An ever growing seed of faith in one's presence and one's reciprocal desire of you.

A feeling not easily found through research or found in the most intimate speech

Love is the center of an atom, most natural and true in unspoken action

Effects on the heart invisible to common man, but seen in the purest of human interaction.

Love is friendship, Love is flexible, Love is faithful.

Through Courtship is the Journey to Love.

A Touch of Heaven

As does heaven, love waits for no one, wake up and get into position.

Intimacy complete without the physical,

the touch in the morning pulling me closer- I yield,

slipping into your tight hold.

Pure connection, I quiver, breathe love on me again.

Creating a refreshing warm breeze, nature stands still to watch in innocent wonder.

My mind and heart collapses with one sigh of surrender.

This is the man who helps me stand tall yet brings me to my knees,

not to degrade rather to submit in thanks for his obedience to God.

He teases my mouth to kiss his lips.

With every kiss you leave protection, with every touch you leave tenderness.

Coming for me as if you thirst to only sip from my cup, paranoid of dehydration

you asked, "fill me up again." I try to catch my breath between each kiss,

your love juice nurturing my existence.

Your deep voice penetrating my mental chords taking me higher, mind lifted above the clouds.

Searching the heavens, I spot the freshness of love,

a white flash of light in darkness.

Your love flows through me as puffs of smoke yet smelling so sweet,

face moist from the dew of your breath.

Torso to torso, my hand to your neck, your hands to my waist and head

to let me fall into l-o-v-e slowly and to keep my eyes on you.

Mental sprints of you when you are not around turning into a slow cross-country walk

when our hearts meet again.

Afraid to close our eyes in fear this moment will disappear you pause and stare,

breast to breast you bow your head in powerless motion to my crown and with a single

tear the staggered beats of your heart spells I l-o-v-e you.

I kiss your stream of joy.

Down by the Sea Shore

Feeling like the seashell tossed in and out of the ocean,
currents ripping at my outer core.
I await in the sand for someone to pick me up,
brush me off and sweep me away with them.

I await to be placed among the other shells
and be called the fairest of them all;
for someone to see my roughness, yet call me soft.
My joy and anticipation rings aloud as crushing waves in my inner core.

Yet, I fear being picked up by one
who cannot be sensitive to my colors, my crevices and my journey.
Instead they step on me, or break me in their hand,
or worst pick me up to treasure then throw me away
for I was worthless compared to the one sought.

Will I ever be desired in love or
die in my dust awaiting, down by the sea shore.

He Is

Strong, dependable...

He is...

Tall and handsome,

skin complexion, I'll leave to the blind.

Blindly guide me to my lover's groove.

Groove me, rock me to your heart

beating forever my lady all night long.

Gazing into each other's eyes

leaves us mesmerized

each by the other's passion

for love and life.

Birthing adventure into our plans,

we discover nature's gifts together.

Together we march among dead roots and

bring living water to dry land offering

prosperity to people.

People see us kiss in committing

our futures to one another.

Another day goes by that I look for you,

my spiritual warrior, my friendly companion, my journey.

He is...

_____

_____

_____

_____

_____

_____

_____

_____

_____

_____

_____

_____

_____

_____

_____

_____

_____

_____

_____

"Love is not a feeling to obtain, but a bridge built on the foundation of faith, hope and trust attempting to bear the weight of two people's journeys."

_____
_____
_____
_____
_____
_____
_____
_____
_____
_____
_____
_____
_____
_____
_____
_____
_____
_____
_____
_____
_____
_____

"Even when love is educated, compassion at times is careless."

"Leaves leaped up and clouds fell when you walked into my life."

Veins of Inspiration

_____

_____

_____

_____

_____

_____

_____

_____

_____

_____

_____

_____

_____

_____

_____

_____

_____

_____

_____

_____

*"You have already won a victory- because the Spirit who lives in you is
greater than the spirit who lives in the world." – 1 John 4:4 (NLT)*

Veins of Inspiration

"Ruin is a gift. Ruin is the road to transformation."
– Elizabeth Gilbert (Eat, Pray, Love)

Veins of Inspiration

"He paces the patterned beats of my heart with every kiss exchanged."

_____

_____

_____

_____

_____

_____

_____

_____

_____

_____

_____

_____

_____

_____

_____

_____

_____

_____

_____

_____

"True passion is to be kissed from the depths of another's soul."

Veins of Inspiration

"I want to live by my heart, not by my flesh."

Veins of Inspiration

"His lips paint my sky with a cloud of kisses."

Veins of Inspiration

"Don't sin by letting anger control you. Think about it overnight and remain silent." – Psalms 4:4 (NLT)

_____
_____
_____
_____
_____
_____
_____
_____
_____
_____
_____
_____
_____
_____
_____
_____
_____
_____
_____
_____

"He kisses me with his heart and holds me with his emotion."

_____
_____
_____
_____
_____
_____
_____
_____
_____
_____
_____
_____
_____
_____
_____
_____
_____
_____
_____
_____
_____
_____

"We cannot think of being acceptable to others until we have
first proven acceptable to ourselves." – Malcolm X

"I knew you when I found you in spirit."

"This is a good sign, having a broken heart. It means we have tried for something." – Elizabeth Gilbert (Eat, Pray, Love)

_____
_____
_____
_____
_____
_____
_____
_____
_____
_____
_____
_____
_____
_____
_____
_____
_____
_____
_____
_____
_____
_____

"My love is for the one who does not exist in my reality."

_____
_____
_____
_____
_____
_____
_____
_____
_____
_____
_____
_____
_____
_____
_____
_____
_____
_____
_____
_____
_____
_____

"He has sent me to heal the brokenhearted...to set at liberty
those who are oppressed." – Luke 4:18 (NKJV)

Veins of Inspiration

_____

_____

_____

_____

_____

_____

_____

_____

_____

_____

_____

_____

_____

_____

_____

_____

_____

_____

_____

_____

_____

"I sought love, I found love, and I indulged in love through age.
I watched my seeds of love take my promise land."

"Love's end has me puzzled and broken into a hundred pieces."

Veins of Inspiration

"A woman desiring fame and fortune will never be satisfied depending on a man's love only."

"*I am sick and tired of people joining together to bring life
to love, only to separate and bring love to death.*"

Veins of Inspiration

"Be a Helen, for to Odysseus she was the strength through his war and breath of his soul." – Inspired by Christopher Marlowe's poem "Helen"

Veins of Inspiration

"If love finds in itself alteration, then could one have truly loved or truly lusted?"

Veins of Inspiration

"A man's love toward a woman will always vary and wilt away like a flower in the winter, it is only when a man finds true love that his love will become constant and bloom like a flower in spring."

Veins of Inspiration

*"That first kiss from the person who you desire the most
will leave its imprint on your lips, with its impact walking in
your mind and heart during your entire life span."*

"Love, it feels like the touch of sunburn in summer and slaps from the piercing wind in winter."

A SPIRITUAL DIALOGUE

I AM that I AM

Who do you say that I am? As I walk by you always with a smile and a glow. Will you see someone trying to radiate through your jaws of life? Or will you look pass my efforts and believe that I am only confused? For to you one should be in sorrow from the suffocating pillows of unfairness in this life. But only would you consider that the very essence of a merry heart does good like medicine. The touch of my friendly hand will I bring to you.

Who do you say that I am? When I feed you "joyful, joyful, Lord we adore thee" in the dwelling of your tears. When I tell you that the melody from your lung's fluctuations make your steps firmer and harder while walking to your task. Will you resound that I'm clueless? Or will you notice that I'm only wise? Opening the book of knowledge will I show you.

Who do you say that I am? When I walk away from your ignorance and your gossip. Will you call me names? Will you consider my namesake within your rumor of lies? Please understand I am not one of pride. But I wear shoes that wherever I am, there blessed quietness and unity shall be in our midst. Who do you say that I am? When you see me often kneel and pray. Will you run away from my corner or will you kneel and join me. Will you call me lost? Or will you realize that I've found a faith that may surpass all understanding. For faith is the confident assurance that what I desire can happen.

Who do you say that I am? When I provide for the banjo player on the market steps with a cup by his side. Or when I sit down on the street to console the poor. Will you call me crazy? Will those of my same standing consider me an embarrassment? Or can you see me offering a chance for those to get off beds of poverty and walk? I am one that believes love and encouragement can conquer a disenfranchised society. For love is never irritable or touchy, never rude or selfish. Love is patient and kind. Will you see me as love when I forgive those that spit on me while I'm sliding along Calvary road, seventy times seven.

Still, who do you say that I am? When you hear me preaching within building walls on the streets, are you listening to my words? Will you consider the meaning of my words worthless or will they be considered useful? What do you think when I say "no weapon formed against you shall prosper?" Will you call me a fake, or will you hearken the phrase minister?

Who do you say that I am? When I carried the weight of your duty on my shoulders, helping you complete your daily chores. Will you call me your strength or take advantage of my being?

Who do you say that I am? Every time I've run to third base to catch you before you were struck out! Every time I opened my heart to your cries of regret! Every time I gave you favor and pleaded for your mercy before many! Do you honestly call me friend, or are you using my generosity to advance yourself in this race? Will you call me warrior every time I had your back in a fight? Will you place me as hero in your war, or will you cut me off from your inheritance? What will I ever be considered to you that I am worthy of being named?

Although I still desire you for myself, "who will you say that I am?"

You were there

In the delivery room, there were complications,
but you were there
because I am.
As a child when I reached for that burning glow,
you were there
and hastened another to take my scar.
In my youth,
struggling to read and calculate,
latent medical conditions unbeknownst to anyone,
you were there to help me concentrate and make the grade.
As I laid on my bed from heartbreaks,
from giving life and having life taken from me
you were there to comfort.
Through family conflict causing confusion and instability,
you told me to speak to the storm with authority.
It passed.
You were there.
In adulthood, I hungered for everyone but you.
I desired your provisions,
in order to continue in my own will.
I ignored your responses,
I cursed you
rather than praised you.
Yet you still listened to me,
you answered every prayer, cry, reasoning and fear.
I am still here, because you were there since the beginning.
Bring back to my heart, my first love – You.
I am because You are.

The Invisible Tangible Love

He is my shadow with clear slight of path, transcending the barriers approaching my front and breaking through the ones holding me back. My anchor, lifting my feet as I walk through a surge of challenges. A home for the mind and body to lay at rest; peace to my troubles, stillness to my labor pains. Rejuvenate me, bring energy to my limbs to work tirelessly for you. Let me stand hand in hand, night to day as you manage mercy. With every drawback and every near touch, I yearn to love you more yet never reaching a heart's satisfaction. Teach me how to depend on you as you hold tightly to me. Take from me what is yours, and only give the experience of you.

Salvation

Are you really ready,
Will you go up there,
Will they look at you strangely,
What will you say,
Do you really believe,
What would you pray for,
Does prayer really work,
What are you supposed to feel afterwards,
Will God really care who you are,
Is he all everyone says he is,
How will life be after you repeat their words,
Is that all you have to do,
How bad of a sinner are you,
How bad of a sinner am I,
If I do wrong again would God want me,
Will he still want you if you do wrong,
Will this lifestyle be difficult,
Is this life worth experiencing,
Are you truly ready for this,
If so, can I come with you?

Purpose Not People

My heart is not meant to love flesh.

Temporary pleasures I take heed in avoiding.

Therefore, I guard my spirit,

my mind and my heart from those things

turning me away from my God-given purpose.

This might sound brash

or you may feel sad for me- please do not,

but try to understand.

My heart does love, but only He or She,

whichever gender you'd like God to be.

Striving everyday to impress one Spirit,

falling and jumping back up,

this path cannot handle much distraction.

Removing other pebbles from my path,

pressing forward until the dream is clear and recognizable,

until action has been taken.

Let no one stand in my way; let me not lose focus,

people are here for a season.

May I reap a harvest as I praise and wave

to those who have placed me on fertile ground.

Oh, Lord

Oh Lord, my guide,
where are you?
I've searched my heart, my mind
yet I cannot find you.
My ears are empty,
my spirit is lacking.
I know I am a sinner,
but I would rather die
than have you turn your boundless back from me.
If I need a daily cleansing- do it Lord.
If I need your daily discipline – give it Lord.
If I need a daily test – send it Lord.
I know nothing so pure except you.
Even when I lose focus,
I yearn to be nearer to you.
I do not know why
I have problems in faithfulness.
But, if it takes me carrying other's tears, sweat, and pain
to show my dedication to you – give it all to me Lord.
I need you more than life's finest things.
Please reveal your love, peace, and joy to me.
Will I ever be satisfied?
Never.
Because the one thing I truly desire
from you is to dwell with you for eternity.

Frightened Wanderer

Speak to my heart...

Awake, my child, connect your spirit with mine.

Meet me at the foot of the bed as I

kiss your forehead gently and hover over you

like a bird soaring in the sky seeking the

mysteries of the heaven's breeze.

Speak to my heart...

Feel my heart as I wrap my spirit

around you so you may hear the

beat of each step you shall take today.

Whether fast or slow my touch is enough to protect.

Speak to my heart...

I have many tasks at hand, but you begin to ponder

feelings of loneliness, a heart with a hollow inside,

ready to give up breath.

My spirit runs to you as a stream makes her path

through rough rocks, only to be let free into a river.

You thirst for a man's touch not mine,

So I allow my spirit to rest as the dew on your mind and heart.

Speak to my heart...

I know the tangible feels more real,

unlike the hopeful touch of the invisible.

Yet the tangible power you see is movable,

unlike the invincible power you cannot see.

My love, dear child, will never change, fail, or burn out.

As you lay and cry in bed,

know that when I hold you in my bosom my love is near.

Speak to my heart...

I say, fear of despair be removed

for the trust of my being should make you glad.

I say, doubt be removed for my works should make you rejoice.

I say loneliness be removed for my warm spirit

should make you blush as a bride.

I am He who speaks to your heart, not only your body.

Be secure and content in my love, for I died and now live for you.

I speak now that you seek my love for you,

before someone else's love for you.

For I speak loyalty to the heart of the frightened wanderer.

A Steady Flow

Saying to myself, someone give me breath on this supposed day of rest,
since speaking out was not my forte.
I went to the building as usual, wondering why this habit hasn't died,
a familiar question.
In obedience to the robe, the congregation offered a workout praise.
One and two-
lift those hands, come on let's see 'em.
Three and four-
raise your voices, come on I can't hear you!
Going with the flow, but not in the flow,
I parted the dirty sea from which my tongue flapped a praise.
Yet it wasn't a praise of thanks, rather "Help Me," was a praise of surrender.
Nervous, as I looked around to see all who were watching,
I closed my eyes
with my fingers I made a knot of hope,
parted the seas and allowed my tongue to flap again
thinking one day this thing will work.
"Help Me."

Then I saw a picture in my mind,
a movie or drawing never known to my thoughts,
yet maybe through the crack in the trapped door of my cold heart.
He was there, in a chair smiling tirelessly.
But someone was leaning on his left knee desperately holding on,
flat affect and looking down, both draped in white gowns.
Odd was the blood streaming from His right foot,
flowing generously under the gown of the man leaning on His left knee.

Opening my eyes, in my view is a man in black and white.
Penguin-like, but on a different warmer mission.
He says, "God may have told us to go right, and at times
we choose to go left, but he forgives and will never forsake you."
My heart and mind immediately connected,
with droplets falling from my scalp and eyes, then flowing across my lips,
I responded, "I believe! I went left, but I am holding on to His knee
desiring His help to never let go."

"True faith faints and recharges."

Veins of Inspiration

_____

_____

_____

_____

_____

_____

_____

_____

_____

_____

_____

_____

_____

_____

_____

_____

_____

_____

_____

_____

"All your life, no one will be able to hold out against you...I'll be with you. I won't give up on you; I won't leave you..." – Joshua 1:5 (MSGV)

Veins of Inspiration

"Faith is taking the first step even when you don't see the whole staircase."
– Dr. Martin Luther King Jr.

Veins of Inspiration

"They are like trees planted along the riverbank, bearing fruit each season. Their leaves never wither, and they prosper in all they do." – Psalms 1:3 (NLT)

Veins of Inspiration

"There is no greater agony than bearing an untold story inside you."
– Maya Angelou

Veins of Inspiration

_____
_____
_____
_____
_____
_____
_____
_____
_____
_____
_____
_____
_____
_____
_____
_____
_____
_____
_____
_____
_____
_____
_____

"Always be joyful. Never stop praying. Be thankful in all circumstances,
for this is God's will for you who belong to Christ Jesus."
– 1 Thessalonians 5:16-18 (NLT)

_____
_____
_____
_____
_____
_____
_____
_____
_____
_____
_____
_____
_____
_____
_____
_____
_____
_____
_____
_____
_____

*"Prejudice is a burden that confuses the past, threatens the future
and renders the present inaccessible." – Maya Angelou*

_____

_____

_____

_____

_____

_____

_____

_____

_____

_____

_____

_____

_____

_____

_____

_____

_____

_____

_____

_____

_____

_____

"In the deserts of the heart let the healing fountain start." – W.H. Auden

Veins of Inspiration

*"I do feel, in my dreaming and yearnings, so undiscovered by
those who are able to help me." – Mary McLeod Bethune*

Veins of Inspiration

"We must use time creatively." – Dr. Martin Luther King Jr.

Veins of Inspiration

"Be still and know that I am God..." – Psalms 46:10 (KJV)

"A genuine leader is not a searcher for consensus but a molder of consensus."
– Dr. Martin Luther King Jr.

Veins of Inspiration

"Therefore, be earnest and disciplined in your prayers." – 1 Peter4:7 (NLT)

Veins of Inspiration

"Nothing in the world is more dangerous than sincere ignorance and conscientious stupidity." – Dr. Martin Luther King Jr.

Veins of Inspiration

"So don't sit around on your hands! No more dragging your feet..."
– Hebrews 12:12 (MSGV)

"We may encounter many defeats but we must not be defeated."
– Maya Angelou

Veins of Inspiration

"If there is no struggle, there is no progress." – Frederick Douglas

_____
_____
_____
_____
_____
_____
_____
_____
_____
_____
_____
_____
_____
_____
_____
_____
_____
_____
_____
_____
_____
_____
_____

"Now all glory to God, who is able to keep you from falling away and will bring you with great joy into his glorious presence without a single fault."
– Jude 1:24 (NLT)

Veins of Inspiration

"We write because we believe the human spirit cannot be tamed and should not be trained." – Nikki Giovanni

Veins of Inspiration

"Real religion...is this: Reach out to the homeless and loveless in their plight, and guard against corruption from the godless world." – James 1:27 (MSGV)

_____
_____
_____
_____
_____
_____
_____
_____
_____
_____
_____
_____
_____
_____
_____
_____
_____
_____
_____
_____
_____
_____

"Don't feel entitled to anything you didn't sweat and struggle for."
– Marian Wright Elderman

_"Let the peace of Christ keep you in tune with each other, in
step with each other...." – Colossians 3:17 (MSGV)_

"The highest result of education is tolerance." – Helen Keller

Veins of Inspiration

"There's a crack (or cracks) in everyone... that's how the light of God gets in."
– Elizabeth Gilbert (Eat, Pray, Love)

SUNDRY THOUGHTS

Weird Science

While in Lab...

He's trying to teach her science, but he has to use psychology.

So he studies her hard and says, "now that's biology."

Giving stare by stare was his ministry, in lustful pleasure she quietly gave the stares back and said, "now that's chemistry."

With every stare he added a touch and with every touch she added a kiss, getting closer to exploring each other's body was the key and they both giddily said, "now that's anatomy."

But then their teacher appeared in their midst and gave them a lesson on the law of passing licks, from a distance he threw two pink slips which glided through the air and landed in front of them. And he said, "now that's the law of physics."

I Call them Survivor

You say you're for right, but you only do wrong.
Hands raised in adoration- to what do you worship?
Spitting fire with smiles,
rain of hatred falling through your gaps
as I advocated for them.
I swerved through isolated spaces
hoping for a cool wind to smooth my burning skin.
Anger in my heart,
skin unravels inside out to see the colored scars on my soul.
I took their place.
Setting free the spirit within me now needing to return,
forgiveness I'll need so cover me with grace before I
interrupt this race to approach your disgrace of a being.
They call you a servant living a calling, but I'm not falling for your lies
they may with their unbridled eyes and affection, needing to be cared for,
vulnerable with one ear open.
You spoke death to them – I spoke life.
Tortured in seeing their demise,
I resigned from this race to join another.
Ultimately hoping to replace their hurt with words of compassion
and offer a hope they will hear with both ears and heart.
Words of wisdom, never to depart from their feet.
Survivor – their new name,
the acclaim to fame for being successful despite
the syringe of negativity forced into their veins.
Now my blood has calmed to see victory in progress,
my hands are raised in adoration to the Creator
for your wrongs have been corrected.

Without

Crumbs without the fulfillment of bread.

A fresh drink without the thirst.

A tree without the soil.

Tears without the emotion.

Goodbyes without the connection of two hearts.

A needle without the pain.

Death without a God.

A chair without a body.

A creative mind without a pen.

Unresurrected

Won't you rise today
and melt me in your warmth.
Will you rise to guide me
through my dark, hectic morning.
Won't you rise today
and teach me why I should never take you for granted again.
Will you rise to give hope to my hopeless spirit.
Won't you rise today
and show me how to be as strong as you.
Will you rise today
and forgive me for insulting you.
Won't you rise today
and stay with me past your curfew.
Will you rise today
so I can return the love past due.
Won't you, will you please
walk in life with me today.

Falling
A Response to Robert Jessup's Painting "Fall" @1986

My life was a bliss, colored with
the kiss from the sun's yellow lips of rays.
The blue skies around me flowed
in sequence with the stretching of the winds.
And fruitful trees followed the seasons
of Mother Nature's plans.
Rocks stayed in their given shape
and place of inferiority.
Life was performing accuracy as an order
given by a king.
And best of all, my dream guy
fell in love with me,
his eyes clear of morning cold, and
filled with afternoon alertness.

But "things aren't always what they appear to be."
Is what I kept hearing from these
eyeless, alien-like figures in the back
of my mind at night, dreaming,
my eyes stuck together from
sweat dripping out of my head due to
frustration brought on by my thoughts.
I kept saying to myself, "life can only be
predictable for innocent people like me."

It all began when the seasons
disagreed with Mother Nature's yearly routines.
My guy started prowling
like a cat at late hours.
I followed him, one day,
like a dog follows a foul sent.
I found two lovers meeting
at our hot spot, in
our special love seat.
What hurts the most is that
all he is was entrapped within me.
I hoped he was only confused like
the splattered expressions on his shirt.

I felt like that inferior rock,
that is easily trampled on.
In that case I wish a book would've
fallen on my head providing insight
to the consequences on love.
I thought about my dream and realized
that I was those eyeless, rejected figures.
And he ran away with nature's order
and trust with his eyes still wide open.

Stopping Traffic

Taking off the Victoria and slipping on the Ann Taylor,
the day is hers to conquer.
She's a silhouette in motion,
fierce and sexy in high heels,
skirt accenting her waist and thighs.
Breasts in position to march to the beat of a new day.
Mind over all matters, she is powerful in every way.
With a flip of the hair she shakes off the morning dew,
the wind's waves visible in her strands.
She switches her hips as if attempting to balance the scales of justice with
every step.
She stops, steps back with a glare, her glare pronounced in mascara smiles
with gratitude,
then forward she clicks her heels back in motion.
Heels not meant to create a physical lie, just two pedestals
to show the world the inside beauty only one man has seen.
Call her conceited, and she shrugs with humble assurance.
Taking off her Ann Taylor and putting on her Victoria,
she says goodbye to the day and the night kisses her to rest
while the world dreams of her grace.

My Brain is Pissed Off

Braids twisted tightly, let my scalp exhale.
Use some botanical shampoo and clean my hair that forest smells.
Bobby pins, clips and crap. OUCH!
God blow the wind so the braids can give her a slap.
Added pieces with glue choke the hell out of me and you.
Wondering why I don't grow, ain't my fault you put me on a diet for a show.
Wouldn't have to subtract if you didn't add.
Pissed Off!
Curly, wavy, straightened, can't we go back to the way we were,
when natural was beautiful and white was her.
Straight to the point, no extra personality,
you were born with creative design, no formalities.
Bottom line, this head is fine,
wash me, leave me alone and watch me praise you.
Pissed off no more,
I told you I would help you stand naturally beautiful and tall.
Air, water, and grease are what I need and that's all.

Build Me A Man

Proctor God, I desire a man
Tall and strong,
handles on hips so I won't fall off,
off this ride of life that I feel when I am with him.
Heaving with elation,
I cry in compensation of this gift that is man,
not just in physique, but manhood exudes his existence.
An MLK, he is a man with a plan to be greater than his last success story.
An Obama, becoming new in his journey with life-filled words to change a classroom,
congregation or nation.
Teaching and preaching revelations not from a silver spoon, but from the fields.
I want a Denzel whose actions are at the playground, heart in the church and head in
the bookstore; swinging me in my childhood bliss as you hold me and talk your
Clinton intelligence, discussing presidential debates,
elect me as your running mate- in life.
My founding father, bringing justice from commonalities,
and exchanging it for deviations from the rules- of love.
A John Cena who speaks victory and not failure as an option.
He is the lawyer who advocates for me when I am right and defends me publically
when wrong, but then objects privately.
Gliding on your wings, you shield me from harsh rains of wrath
when I don't see the consequences of my actions, you are my bulwark.
A man who won't take the first shiny apple that falls from the tree, but waits till
each falls to inspect them cautiously,
protecting oneself from foolish love that fails.
Emotions not like the leaves vacillating in the wind, rather you stand firmly positioned
as the bark on a tree,
I rip at your exterior and your character remains strong.
He is the chef, creativity not contingent upon recipes,
his only ingredient is love presented in all forms.
Dripping into a pot of his love, he is the waiter who serves me another bowl,
I tip him with submission.
Drink again my King from this cup.
Create in him a heart of a David, able to take control of his home and family with the
holding of hands and bowed heads,
favor walks with me because he talks with thee.

Creator God, build me a man.

Breathing life into me revealing a creation of our physicality inside of me I give birth to fellow man.

Enclose me in your womb, growth of love for me you express in your delivery of strength in pain and patience during disaster.

You show me the beauty of creation once so scared to experience,

but you bring me back to basics, my country's need of survival.

I desire the construction worker, no fragrance needed,

but the sweat of a day's labor.

A man called to rebuild and refurbish yet often disrespected, ridiculed and abused, you walk Calvary's way with a nail in one hand and hammer in another expecting to restore what you truly desire- love.

My wall of protection, lullaby me into a dream,

safely I rest in your haven.

Put no one after or before, you are all encompassing of my world, a gift from God.

Self-sufficient alone, but with you I'd rather be conjoined.

Reflecting smiles, he is my pillar through weathering.

A comedian, laughing me through the rough sides of the mountain, giggles ranging from valleys high and valleys low, I'm content in his comfort and security.

My garbage disposal, you take all I dump onto you

carrying me without throwing me away.

My Terrance Howard, your tunnels shine as the lighthouse,

without the script, you portray concern for me when I go and when I come.

My Moses, your spirit is with me in travels.

I fall on your chocolate earth.

Nourish and mold me into a new lover;

like an LL Cool J, his love is like cool jelly.

There is credit in your kisses no withdrawal

simply fast cash to keep me desiring more.

The only lieutenant I'll walk behind whose shadow steps aside to let me shine.

When I march off, lick and fold me like an envelope.

Flexibility of a Brown, yet more in words.

Just remember when I leave impress return to giver on my heart.

You hold the remedy for every ailment, operating just by your presence.

A Randy Orton, I am your tag team partner in life and death.

Once dead yet alive again when you found me, sought me and

claimed me as your patient.

Merciful God, prepare this man for me.
We will live on a trajectory with no tracks just air,
Jordan has nothing on you.
You save a slam-dunk for the 4th quarter,
my coach stretching me to achieve more greatness,
it sometimes hurts but always works.
Like A1 sauce in my steak, smooth toughness laid on me
like butter on my biscuits you moisture with your bountiful lips.
A masterpiece; Van Gogh, Marcus Glenn,
reflect classic yet color in their style.
My Greek reality, poetry is in your form,
music in your walk.
Spirits align;
we walk in one soul,
let the world see our love.
One plus one will equal just one,
our equation makes no sense to the human eye,
but only to God's masterful plan.
God I am ready, send me my man.

Wasting Time

The wind zapped our faces like electricity,
the wooden gates swinging,
in front of our home, tall and pointed,
mother walked us inside casually.

We ate dinner casually,
our speech competing with the thunder's electricity,
dad stepped away from the table and pointed,
to the jukebox, and started swinging.

He said fear of storms is calmed by swinging,
my mother laughed casually,
her voice cracking like electricity,
I gazed at them with my eyebrows upward pointed.

Toward them my feet tapped and pointed,
they took my hands casually,
my body started swinging,
my skirt rising above static electricity.

Sounds of electricity,
starts us swinging,
our feet toward the music pointed,
with hips and clothes twirling casually.

Veins of Inspiration

*"Poetry is not the art of language, but dispelling
the truth inherent in unspoken words."*

_____

_____

_____

_____

_____

_____

_____

_____

_____

_____

_____

_____

_____

_____

_____

_____

_____

_____

_____

_____

_____

"God keeps your days stable and secure-salvation, wisdom
and knowledge in surplus." – Isaiah 33:6 (MSGV)

"One man's order is another man's confusion; nothing is ever perfect, just like how the clouds constantly reconfigure shapes in the sky; within order there is always a hint of disorder."

Veins of Inspiration

"Abundance is, in large part, an attitude."
– Sue Patton Thoele, The Women's Book of Confidence

"Why strive to win a trophy that only reflects your acting when you can have a plaque that reflects your true spirit."

_____
_____
_____
_____
_____
_____
_____
_____
_____
_____
_____
_____
_____
_____
_____
_____
_____
_____
_____
_____
_____
_____
_____
_____

"Walk straight, act right, tell the truth." – Psalms 15:2 (MSGV)

Veins of Inspiration

"Never become so much of an expert that you stop gaining expertise.
View life as a continuous learning experience." – Denis Waitley

184

Veins of Inspiration

"I've learned that you can't have everything and do everything at the same time." – Oprah Winfrey

_____

_____

_____

_____

_____

_____

_____

_____

_____

_____

_____

_____

_____

_____

_____

_____

_____

_____

_____

_____

_____

"To everything there is a season and a time to every purpose
under the heavens." – Ecclesiastes 3:1 (KJV)

"A man may fall many times but he won't be a failure until he says someone pushed him." – Elmer G. Letterman

"After every spiritual test there's a promotion, but you can't get the promotion before you go through the test. Some of you are in a test for your legacy and family." ~ Pastor Harold B Hayes Jr.

Veins of Inspiration

_____
_____
_____
_____
_____
_____
_____
_____
_____
_____
_____
_____
_____
_____
_____
_____
_____
_____
_____
_____
_____
_____

"Four steps to achievement: Plan purposefully. Prepare prayerfully.
Proceed positively. Pursue persistently." – William A Ward

Veins of Inspiration

"Learn your ABC's- Abilities Beyond Circumstances"

"Loneliness is not the absence of people; it's the absence of one's own identity."

_____

_____

_____

_____

_____

_____

_____

_____

_____

_____

_____

_____

_____

_____

_____

_____

_____

_____

_____

_____

"Don't look out for your own interests, but take an interest in others too."
– Philippians 2:4 (NLT)

"Fear is only beneficial when it causes to you to fight for your life."

Veins of Inspiration

"Be careful about reading health books. You may die of a misprint."
– Mark Twain

Veins of Inspiration

_____
_____
_____
_____
_____
_____
_____
_____
_____
_____
_____
_____
_____
_____
_____
_____
_____
_____
_____
_____
_____
_____
_____

"I know what I'm doing. I have it all planned out – plans to take care of you, not abandon you, plans to give you the future you hope for."
– Jeremiah 29:11 (MSGV)

Veins of Inspiration

"Everyone has inside of him a piece of good news! The good news is that
you really don't know how great you can be, how much you can love,
what you can accomplish and what your potential is." - Anne Frank

Veins of Inspiration

"If you don't learn how to let stuff go, you are walking dead."
– Co-Pastor Kellie V. Hayes

"Do the one thing you cannot do. Fail at it. Try again. Do better the second time. The only people who never tumble are those who never mount the high wire. This is your moment. Own it." – Oprah Winfrey

"Prophesy and speaking in unknown languages and special knowledge will become useless. But love will last forever!" – 1 Corinthians 13:8 (NLT)

_____

_____

_____

_____

_____

_____

_____

_____

_____

_____

_____

_____

_____

_____

_____

_____

_____

_____

_____

"I would rather die envisioning my ideal than walk through life settling."

Veins of Inspiration

"There is nothing as remarkable as learning how to think better."- Anonymous

Veins of Inspiration

"Sow a thought, and you reap an act; sow an act, and you reap a habit; sow a habit, and you reap a character; sow a character, and you reap a destiny."
– Charles Reade

About the Author

Jennifer Gillyard was born and raised in Philadelphia, Pennsylvania. She is a graduate of the University of Virginia and received a Masters of Science in Social Work from Columbia University. At the age of 27, Jennifer is pursuing a Masters of Divinity at Wesley Theological Seminary. Jennifer plans to use her education to practice Social Work internationally and conduct research in Ecumenism and Interreligious Dialogue.

Jennifer began writing poetry as a child at the age of 12 years old and wanted to write this book to share her journey as a poet, woman, and lifelong child at heart. Other than poetry, Jennifer is passionate about serving children and families in disadvantaged communities. She is a licensed minister pursuing ordination in the African Methodist Episcopal Church. She volunteers her time with her church Hunter Memorial AME, Habitat for Humanity, and the Congressional Black Caucus. In Jennifer's spare time, she enjoys travelling, spending time with friends, watching the *WE* Channel or WWE Wrestling and cheering for UVA and Philadelphia sports teams.

Jennifer resides in Alexandria, Virginia.